METAPHYSICAL MAXIMS

ENLIGHTENMENT through
MEDITATION & MORALS

J.R. Azizollahoff

ISBN 0-7414-4771-1

Published by:

INFINITY
PUBLISHING.COM
1094 New DeHaven Street, Suite 100
West Conshohocken, PA 19428-2713
Info@buybooksontheweb.com
www.buybooksontheweb.com
Toll-free (877) BUY BOOK
Local Phone (610) 941-9999
Fax (610) 941-9959

Printed in the United States of America

Printed on Recycled Paper

Published May 2009

Dedication

To my brothers, Daniel & Victor, my wife, Li Kwang,
& daughter, Naomi

Acknowledgments

I wish to thank my late teacher of ethics, Mr. Shamariah
Yohananoff, for cultivating my adamant belief in morality in
1978. I thank God for making me open to my teacher's ideas
while drifting aimlessly in materialism many years ago.
While my approach to Spirit differs from his, I am indebted to
Mr. Yohananoff for putting me on the road to Truth as well.

I also wish to thank the hundreds of authors, philosophers,
theologians, rabbis, ministers, and mystics whose words
and writings helped me to achieve my understanding of Being
and virtue.

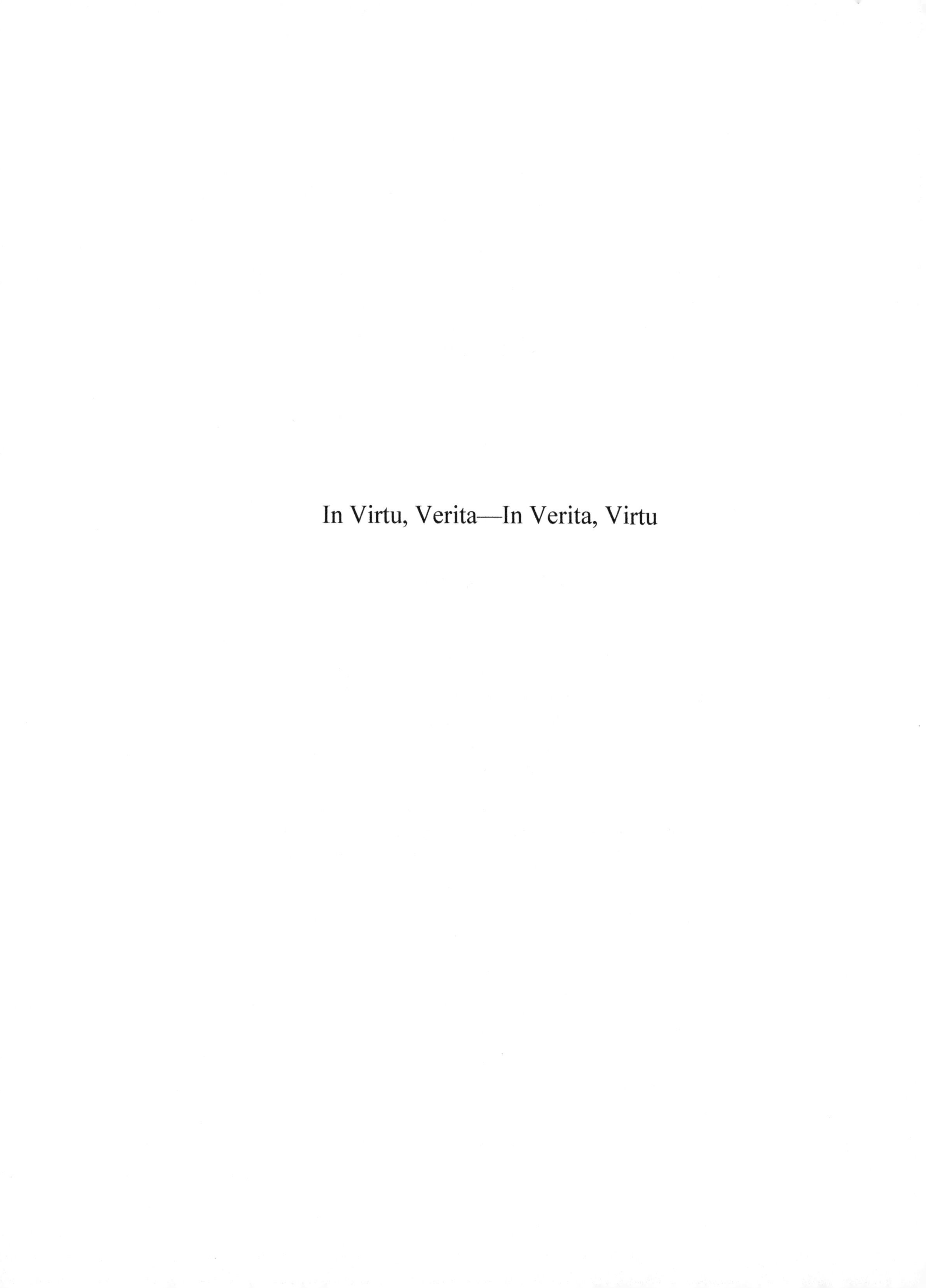

In Virtu, Verita—In Verita, Virtu

Sections

1. Metaphysics: Truth, Spirit, or the Present

1. Get into the Wisdom of the ages: Be here Now.

2. The Present is the best present one can receive.

3. Metaphysical synonyms include Peace, Way, Truth, Life, Love, Wisdom, Now, Present, God, Reality, Spirit, Holy Spirit, Being, and Mind.

4. The Now is the substance of all that does not contain physical quantity, and the reality of everything that is not matter.

5. As you begin to understand the invalidity of the material world, you develop a taste for Reality.

6. Seeing is believing particularly when you are observing the Spirit.

7. Truth is, was, and shall be forever.

8. The ignorant ignore the Now.

9. An ounce of Spirit is far more substantive than a pound of matter, or Spirit is greater than matter to the nth power.

10. People who need people are the luckiest people in the world if they use their God given delicacy as a spur to seek the Spirit.

11. The Now is sacred silence, and it is sacrilegious, and paradoxical, to talk or write about it too much.

12. Within and about us is that which is more precious than anything else on earth; the only caveat is that it cannot be seen or touched, only witnessed.

13. A good day is one in which you find yourself in Being a good deal of the time; on a bad day you are lost in imagination and activity all the time.

14. Progress is being made when the fellowship of the Holy Spirit becomes more natural, comfortable, and familiar.

15. Everyone can have a love in their life: The Now.

16. The only external worth thinking about is God.

17. The desire to possess a beautiful thing is a futile or self-contradictory attempt to bottle or own the Present that does not exist in the form of an article; the object becomes boring after a while because the Now neither is, nor ever was, to be found in it.

18. We are greeted by the Present at least several times a day, and must seize upon those precious moments when we move out of time, and expand upon them, for as long as possible.

19. To be clear and avoid confusion, maintain good values that are never compromised, and meditate out all the negativity, until the small mind is purged, and the greater Mind remains.

20. We are not surrounded by air, but the Spirit; breathe in the Spirit, and become a spiritual person.

21. Have Being, not the last word.

22. When one is fully seeped in Being tears may well in the eyes, for the beauty and the glory of the Now.

23. To be or not to be is not the question, for Being is the

answer, in this and the next worlds.

24. After an hour of complete interactive and reactive nonsense, a moment of long-awaited Reality bursts into consciousness, and gives us much needed relief and comfort.

25. Make the figure in one's life God or Being, and the ground the workaday world of sensation and materialism.

26. The purpose of a book, that is material, is to negate itself, so that we can see beyond its physical surface to the immaterial world of Reality.

27. What is called, "Classic", in art, craft, or design, is a beautiful object that exudes Being around itself, when viewed by an observer.

28. You know you are entering into the glory of the Now when your awareness of the Present begins to intrude upon the pictures and thoughts that float through the mind to such a degree that you are no longer a slave of the past or future.

29. The Now is the best life has to offer, and all who have experienced it for prolonged periods agree that all else is just second rate.

30. Persist in the Present.

31. Be moderate in everything, except the love of God.

32. The price of the Present is the ego.

33. The more one grows in Love, Peace, or Being the more sympathetic one becomes to the anger and violence of others, and the less likely one will react with hostility to the bad actions of others.

34. Great meaning in life can be gained from one's work or profession, but the greatest meaning can only be derived from

self-awareness or consciousness of the Now.

35. A job should not be a place for ego validation, or a place where you prove to yourself how great you are, for our real selves are only validated by God, the source of our being.

36. Never neglect the Now.

37. Give up your petty desires in the knowledge that the Present is all that you know, and ever need know, now and forever.

38. Believe in the Truth that sets man free, and not dogmas, or spiritual materialism.

39. The meaning of life is the Truth that sets one free and nothing more, and the wise should not obfuscate this simple fact.

40. If you must remember, remember the Present, and all the wonderful times you had as a consequence of it.

41. If you catch a real glimpse of Love, God, Spirit, greater Mind, or the Now, you will never be the same again, and you will want to help others experience Peace and power.

42. Nothing can defeat the Present, for the Now, or God, always defeats the devil, in the form of the past or future.

43. The Now is the seer as the seen, and the observer as the observed; we withdraw from the observed world as we view ourselves observing it.

44. Be filled with the Present moment; be supplied by the indwelling of the Holy Spirit.

45. In order to understand the superiority of the Now to thought, one must find it out for oneself, for no one can explain it intellectually, as it can only be known existentially.

46. Believe in the Now and achieve Life now and hereafter.

47. Anger is reduced by Spirit; thus the seeker should react less when troubled people, who are unfortunately entirely in imagination, and not privy to Reality, criticize her.

48. The Present protects us from pain.

49. If the Present is with us, how can the past or future be against us?

50. Hold onto the Present, the lifeboat of the mind.

51. Problems are good if they bring us closer to God.

52. Regardless of what happens in our lives, good or bad, we should all remember that we have more pressing issues, namely, to seek the Present moment, our perennial escape from the exigencies of the material world.

53. If someone may have cheated or taken advantage of you in a small way, try not to discover that it has happened, because it is irrelevant to a life in Reality or Spirit.

2. Enlightenment

1. People will try anything to achieve the beatific vision, except the cessation of all activity.

2. It is better to bask, than ask, for Enlightenment.

3. Animals can move and feel, and man can move, feel, think, and create, but the enlightened try to avoid these activities, when possible.

4. A slight or even fairly significant disability is a small price to pay for Illumination.

5. The Divine Science is an attempt to bring us back to our primordial spiritual beginnings by overcoming the ill effects of language.

6. Romance languages that are rapidly spoken slow the process of Illumination that requires action to be reduced in intensity and speed, including the spoken word.

7. Many people know a lot more about Enlightenment than the enlightened, but are not spiritual at all.

8. If you are on the road to Truth and virtue, and someone mired in materialism hates and is rude to you, consider it their, rather than your, loss.

9. The truly pure and harmless have tremendous strength and power, but never use it against others, under almost all circumstances.

10. Once you can go into your Shangri- La at will, you will be more agreeable to others, as you say to yourself, "They can

say or think as they wish, but I am going back to my oasis now."

11. The only way to find your way is through the Way.

12. Reading the right books can help on the path to Illumination, but after Enlightenment is achieved, reading becomes more of a superfluous distraction, as Peace is sought for its own sake, and Love begins to bloom in the heart of man.

13. In order to make something of oneself, metaphysically, in life, one should start around the age of twenty five, or at about the same time as one begins vocational training, for life is too short to make significant progress in the Way, if one begins the search for Reality too late in life.

14. The enlightened have little interest in money, fame, or power, considered by the materialist to be the ultimate aphrodisiacs, because they always have access to ecstasy, just as soon as they close their eyes, or look up in the sky.

15. As you progress in the Way, and begin to enjoy the Now, you may appear to others as a little preoccupied, or perhaps even unfriendly, so it is important to engage people in congenial conversation, and keep proper appearances, with love, and never condescension.

16. Regardless of how they feel about others on a personal or ego level, the enlightened are on speaking terms with everyone.

17. The first step toward Enlightenment is to join a church or other established religious institution, in order develop a minimal sense of order, self-restraint, and virtue in one's life.

18. A betrayal, illness, mental breakdown, sudden loss of money, or other shock that leads to a giant step forward toward Illumination, but does not result in serious mental or

physical injury, is a blessing in disguise.

19. The enlightened are not without a degree of psychosomatic anxiety, caused by the ego's attempts to ground the soul in the material world, as it attempts to soar upward, or merge with God.

3. Happiness or Peace

1. The greatest happiness you ever had is the same as your joy right now, if you only stop, close your eyes, and feel it.

2. If you do not feel great right now, you fail to understand that this is as good as it gets.

3. All men are created equal, but not all have equanimity.

4. We think that special moment was when we experienced a particular person or place in a wondrous way, but it was the Present, at that precise time, that was the source of the inexplicable joy that we remember so well.

5. The mystic blocks out the fear of death through bliss, and the belief that his soul will finally return to the great sea of Being, that he loves so much, again one day.

6. Rest on your laurels, if they consist of your capacity to rest.

7. Disturbance occurs when the self is not remembered or observed; the price of Peace is constant vigilance in which the observer is the observed.

8. Notice those short times during the day when there is internal and external Peace, and realize that these are the high points of the day, and not just moments that should be avoided at all costs.

9. Procrastination is the proof of Life.

10. Madness or mania often involves moving fast, and talking quickly to oneself, and that is why we try to be still, and not say anything.

11. Many people correctly believe in eye- opening, life-changing experiences, but few know that the ultimate goal of these encounters is Peace.

12. Give Peace a chance: stop protesting, rest your mind, and be a positive example for others in your own vicinity.

13. Long for an end to yearning.

14. Most people have pleasurable, peaceful feelings when alone, but they do not know that they are only experiencing a tiny morsel of the bliss that is possible for those who seek deeper, and more permanent, levels of tranquility.

15. Animals are defined by their circumstances, or nature, permanently and completely, from which they cannot escape; man is the only animal that can voluntarily withdraw from sensation to live a life of Peace.

16. Because he does not know what the ideal world of Peace and space is, the rationalist secular pagan is in abject fear of death, when his vaunted ego, that he cherishes so much, is destroyed, whereas the mystic does not feel that the final loss of the ego is such a bad idea after all.

17. There is always time in our busy workaday world to do absolutely nothing.

18. Self enhancement ideally should be from enhancing or being enhanced by the greater Self around us, not from a reaction to transient material or external causes, such as praise or admiration.

19. Marriages often fail when one partner stops reacting to the other's reactions, and realizes that he or she has reached a higher level of life, and prefers tranquility to conflict.

20. Housework, a sore point in most marriages, is one of the most spiritual and mindful activities, and no one should complain about this wonderful oasis, in the midst of life's transient concerns.

21. Live in that wonderful, insulated, eternal cocoon of silent space.

22. If you cannot stop, at least try to slow down a little in life, and then slowly learn to cease all action, mental and physical.

23. After you have spoken your peace to yourself, sub vocally, gaze at a pleasant object and sense true Peace for a while.

24. Indulge yourself in the Present, and have greater happiness than when you are out of it.

25. Allow others to express themselves emotionally or politically, agree with them politely, and do not react, for purposes of external and internal tranquility; go along to get along, with utmost sincerity, for this is comity, a positive value.

26. Many are hostile to those who can stop and step out of time because of jealousy, and the belief that tranquility is impossible for them to attain; a better response is to have a little humility, and ask the advanced seeker how he or she was able to stop all activity, and achieve Peace.

27. Ravines, glades, gorges, meadows, glens, valleys, canyons, flat lands, deserts, mountains, and lakes are useful aides in the quest for Peace.

28. Utter calm, simplicity, and quiescence, are often the best examples of virtue, and give guidance to others in many positive and unknown ways.

29. Equanimity is reacting calmly and patiently to a lack of service for a long time, rather than just a few minutes, even if one has other things to do.

30. Happy are those who know, existentially, that the greater Mind conquers all.

31. One cannot remember anything bad if one remembers one's self.

32. It is not time but tranquility that heals all wounds.

33. In order to live in Peace and Love one must strive to achieve the stolidity of God through meditation.

4. Wisdom & Philosophy

1. Facts integrate into knowledge, and knowledge becomes categorized into understanding, which ultimately leads to Wisdom; Wisdom is Truth, but those who continue to study have not achieved it, for if they did, they would stop seeking it.

2. Real psychology is nothing less than Reality, not verbal mumbo jumbo.

3. Man is always striving, and most western philosophers correctly understood that this is suffering, but they did not understand that beneath this struggle is the Peace that transcends our understanding.

4. The chief error of western philosophy was the belief that the Now or Present moment is bad rather than bliss.

5. The greatest philosophers of the East and West knew that the primary object of their search was Spirit.

6. The end of philosophy, religion, and history lies in the unification of morality and Spirit.

7. Philosophy is the handmaid to religion, and religion is the bridesmaid to Enlightenment, as abstraction still grounded in thought evolves into transcendence.

8. The old adage, "Still waters run deep", means that deep thinkers are silent.

9. Philosophy is the use of words to explain something that cannot be understood with words.

10. To avoid a life of mere rationalization for all manner of behavior, one must reflect upon oneself dispassionately.

11. It is better to be impoverished and know something, than have fame and fortune and know nothing.

12. A person's worth is based upon his values and spiritual development only, and not his race, office, wealth, or other material things.

13. All have heard about meditation and morality so we are without excuse, and will be judged, if only by natural law, if we refuse to look into concentration and virtue as the two great cornerstones of life.

14. If people get together and do not discuss moral and spiritual development, or practical personal matters, they are left only with atomistic materialism, in a million different disguises.

15. The purpose of philosophy or religion is to get you to the point where you do not have to philosophize, pray, or study anymore.

16. The philosophical quest is, ironically, not a search for knowledge, but Truth, Being, or Reality.

17. Some western philosophers understood Reality, but explained it in a manner that no one could understand; the Present is the epitome of abstraction, which is intuitively experienced, and is only confused when explained in an abstract, intellectual manner.

18. Better to be poor and know that a circle is a circle, than rich and believe that a circle is a square.

19. The lowest level of life is that of the quid pro quo or reciprocity in which one only helps someone who assists

oneself; but progress begins when benevolence replaces mutual back washing.

20. A most important goal is to know about the paramount things in life, for many people have a lot, but very few have Wisdom, a more precious commodity.

21. If a person has greater intelligence, she has a better capacity to solve problems, but also, unfortunately, to defend her ego.

22. It is more important to be wise than smart.

23. The solution to the riddle of the ages, or the answer to the perennial question, "What is Wisdom?", or "What is life all about?" is answered only by stillness.

24. The stillness required in order to experience the Wisdom of the ages is generally found in those who learn to restrain their aggressiveness, and are considerate to others.

25. Most youth today feel that their life is without meaning if they do not have romantic involvements, when in reality, the lack of romance is a blessing, as it frees one to concentrate on the most important things in life: moral and spiritual development.

26. People imagine they are great because they can do X, Y, or Z, but are truly majestic if they neither imagine nor do anything at all.

27. The beginning of Wisdom is the increased consideration for others, or courtesy.

28. Corporal punishment of children for major transgressions, such as disrespect toward parents, administered dispassionately, is a necessity.

29. The hardest part of raising a child is discipline, for

responsible parents require strength and courage to make a juvenile cry, if necessary; if a child is not trained, it grows up ignorant, and is thus susceptible to bad influences or predators.

30. The only way for children to be accountable for their actions is for their parents to be accountable to God's moral laws.

31. If people knew that on the level of ego they were not good, they would not regret their superficial mistakes in life.

32. The question is not so much how long you have lived, but how far you have evolved in the time allotted, and how many people you have helped and supported, including your closest loved ones, while you were here.

33. Great people, such as Gandhi or Martin Luther King, were very forgiving because they understood people, without condescension, and were not surprised by their hostile behavior, when it was displayed or revealed.

34. The excessive tolerance and insufficient discipline of children characteristic of the valueless '60's generation is the exact opposite of the universal Love, and gentleness, of the psychically evolved, because Love is not motivated by the need to be loved by people, but the desire to support others, freely and without conditions, and, as a consequence, to receive the Love of God.

35. The previous generation negated the better values of their forefathers, and this generation, to be reborn, must negate the negation of their parents.

36. Correct the ignorant, or morally deprived, and he is indignant; admonish the wise and he is calm and thankful.

37. What good is it to earn millions, and not know how to talk

to people in a civilized manner, or how not to talk at all?

38. Better betrayed than betrayer.

39. Be dedicated, not consecrated, to your employer.

40. Small "b" being attracts its own level of being; if, over time, one person's being increases more than the other, magnetism is diminished.

41. The capacity to fight to defend your self is an important aspect of inner power, derived from the essential experience of having fought in the sandbox as a child, but greater valor is required to take on more responsibility such as raising a family.

42. Teach your child that the secret of life is to be a good person, and to try to love others as much as possible.

5. Meditation

1. The only thing we can be certain is never a waste of time is meditation.

2. Thoughtfulness is obliviousness; mindfulness is Reality.

3. Less is more, but the most is nothing.

4. The easiest way to lose the desirable capacity to observe or remember your self is to start talking or listening to someone.

5. Although one does not intend to be vengeful, self-awareness is, inadvertently, the best revenge.

6. A person may be excellent at meditation, with a highly concentrated and focused mind, but may not appreciate his superb mental capacity, like a man sitting on a pot of gold, unaware of the treasure that surrounds him.

7. Our eyes are covered by scales that prevent God's light from reaching the soul, but we must help Him remove these barriers through concentration and meditation.

8. Man is meant to gaze, not graze.

9. We are like small, inert, moving planets, frittering away the energy of the universe; if we stop, and remain completely still, we harness more energy, are empowered, and become stars.

10. To be fairly still is not a simple matter, but to be like a stone is more difficult.

11. If you could see yourself more, you could save your soul and eyesight at the same time.

12. If someone calls you a statue or potted plant, take it as a compliment and a sign of progress.

13. The best, or most valid, excuse for lateness is that one was lost in Being a little too long.

14. Meditation is time best spent, and heals all problems and maladies, mental or physical.

15. Meditate with tenacity, and persist, seated with eyes closed, and back erect, until the spaces between thoughts are lengthened, and begin to dominate one's consciousness.

16. Whether it takes months or years, continue to meditate and never despair, because this is the best way to achieve Peace, Truth, or Love.

17. Close your eyes and let the blackness push all sickness out of your mind, heart, and body.

18. Lie comfortably on your right side in bed, breathe knowingly, relax, and have a very restful meditation.

19. Stand erect, head facing forward, and hold the position, while remembering your self, for about five minutes, and increase the time gradually, as time permits.

20. One can always meditate with eyes opened for long periods by viewing plants, bushes, trees, and grass, for green is the most restful color, as it is at the center of the color spectrum.

21. Look at everything, all at once, without categorization or discernment, and you will experience transcendence; by not labeling the material world, the spiritual world, that should also not be classified, is known.

22. There are three fundamental active ways to transcend: all seeing or total simultaneous perception without identification or categorization, single distant object observation, and self-observant breathing.

23. The only problem with meditating while waiting on line is that you must eventually reach your destination, and reenter the material world.

24. Meditate, enter the real world, and be remanded into God's custody on your own recognizance.

25. In the meditative state, one knows that God is the alpha and omega of life, and is all and everything, both omnipotent and omnipresent; there is no space for the devil in this environment.

26. Heretofore, there has been the belief that meditation was only possible with the eyes closed, peering off the tip of one's nose, or concentrating upon the center of one's forehead; effective meditation can occur anywhere– in a shopping mall, coffee shop, or while walking, provided one can gently focus at or above ground level, or upon an object in the distance.

27. Great writers have rhapsodized about the beauty of nature from time immemorial; the idea, however, is to meditate upon it.

28. Try to wash, dress, eat, walk, and do simple mechanical work in mental silence.

29. Meditate your way to a most memorable nonobjective and rarefied experience, with no extraneous concrete referents worth remembering.

30. Poor being or substance results in excessive sensation, and in order to get off the treadmill of materialism, one must meditate one's way to better being.

31. Initially, when you fix your gaze upon a distant object, thoughts may rush through the mind unawares, but by retaining the pose, thoughts slow down, and eventually stop altogether; this is a blessed event for all who have sufficient tenacity to overcome mendacity.

32. The large, deep landscape painting, with great breadth and scope, is one of the least materialist physical objects, and may be meditated upon for several minutes, without mental strain.

33. Photography freezes the moment, removes us from time, and gives us a sense of the greater Being around us.

34. Misty old Chinese and Japanese scroll paintings allow the viewer to deeply meditate upon the landscape, and may be useful in achieving a peaceful state of mind.

35. Monet's large water lily paintings are translucent and restful, and are thus good objects of meditation.

36. A contemporary abstract painting, with beautiful translucent colors, may be a helpful for meditation, provided you can focus upon it for as long as possible, with a relaxed mind.

37. Abstract painting can enhance being for brief, but not insignificant, periods of time, and remind us of God, or the healing Present.

38. An artwork is useful not so much as an object, but as a springboard that helps the viewer withdraw from the senses, into the Spirit or Being that surrounds him.

39. Meditate upon, rather than briefly observe, the beautiful colors of flowers, and soothing power of green leaves, and grass for as long as time permits.

40. The apathy or impassivity of meditation, ironically, leads to sympathy for others, for Love is the consequence, or equivalence, of Peace, and a reflection of God's stolidity.

41. If your mind feels a little strain while looking at an agreeable object, move your eyes to another, and concentrate upon it for as long as you are comfortable, and then refocus on something else, for a beneficial meditation.

42. People can only gaze for a few moments because of buffers, or mental blockages, but with practice and persistence, all can break through the barriers, and see the light of God, or the Truth that sets man free.

43. In order to temporarily eliminate thought when in the shower, meditate by sensing the water running off the top of your head, for the mind is a more terrible thing to waste than a little water.

44. Try to walk without looking at others, or material objects, by looking down at a spot about fifteen feet in front of you, while looking up occasionally to see where you are going.

45. One only makes real progress in the Way when one learns to love the magnificent blackness that one sees when the eyes are closed more than anything else in the world.

46. Close your eyes, bask your face in the sun on a park bench, and feel the warmth of the greater Being around you; then go home, sit on your sofa, and try to have the same experience for as long as possible.

47. Gawk like a hawk.

48. As you sit, breathe, focus on a distant object, and concentrate; as you stand, or while you walk, follow the same procedure.

49. The way to the Spirit is through an elongated rectangle formed by our eyes and an object in the distance.

50. Provided there are not too many lights, ceilings are wonderful places of repose for the mind, and with practice can foster a magnificent meditation, for those who would but take the time to look up and concentrate.

51. The goal of meditation is the reduction of mental pictures, or imagination; the obverse is madness, the trauma of continuous irrational, disordered, and terrifying pictorialization.

52. If one stands or sits alone, and focuses the mind, others often become nervous, think that you must be going crazy, and start to engage you in conversation that you do not need or want at this time.

53. Broaden your mind by looking at the widest vista, or most spacious panoramic view, such as a large lake with mountains in the background, or a plateau with a gaping view for miles around in all directions.

54. One should meditate away, but never act out, the pain of the past.

55. A good job, for those who can afford it, will not excessively interfere with a modest meditation.

56. If you are meditating in public, move your head from time to time, so as not to arouse the suspicion that you are crazy, or visiting from another planet.

57. Serenity through meditation heals over stimulation, the cause of so many diseases.

6. Breathing

1. Bliss is sensing the slight up and down movement of the ribs as you breathe.

2. If you know how to breathe with awareness, you know a lot more than intellectuals who have read thousands of books.

3. The ears were meant for listening to one's breathing.

4. To deflate the ego, inflate the lungs.

5. The more you consciously breathe while on earth, the more likely you will continue to remain conscious after death.

6. No amount of wealth is worth the price of conscious breathing.

7. You only know you are living when you know you are breathing.

8. Sit or stand with good posture, and cotton in your ears to make breathing more audible; close your eyes, experience the blackness, and listen to your breathing at the same time, for as long as possible.

9. Because it is so joyful, mindful breathing obviates the need to react to the criticism of others.

10. Conscious breathing is one of the easiest ways to get to the Now.

11. If you wish, you may vary your breathing, and hold your breath from time to time during meditation.

12. If you want to find your self, discover your breath as it enters your lungs, for Spirit equals breath plus observation.

13. We, the walking dead, can only be resuscitated by conscious breathing.

14. Breathing is the hydraulic brake of the human machine, but people always accelerate, or at best coast at high speed, and wonder why they keep hitting things.

15. Let others have their way with you, and have the last word, as you simply keep and enjoy your little secret: conscious, rhythmic breathing.

16. Anxiety, or unconscious, shallow breathing, is instantaneously cured by conscious, rhythmic breathing.

17. Conscious breathing heals physical illness as it brings more fresh oxygen to the lungs and heart.

18. Because they do not know how to consciously breathe the air around them, people are bottom feeders on the ocean floor of materialism.

7. Stillness

1. Stop, stand straight, look at a distant object, breathe attentively and rhythmically, and try to appear like a Greek or Roman statue, a motionless mime, or a figure in a wax museum.

2. The best game to play with your child is to see who can stand or sit still for the longest time.

3. The beatific vision of the great Catholic saints is the capacity to strike a prolonged meditative pose, concentrating totally upon loving God, for as long as one wishes, at any time one wants.

4. Provided everything stops, including thought, one realizes that doing nothing always makes one happier than doing something.

5. It is easy to work and sleep, but hard to stop and rest.

6. Although most do not understand why they love them so much, beautiful prints, paintings, and home accents exhibit the power of Being, stillness, or the Present.

7. Just occupy a seat.

8. The good life is one in which you sit or stand still, and breathe normally, and consciously.

8. Clouds

1. The cloud is the most abstract physical quantity in the visible world, and as such can be viewed, at length, without the ill effects of materialism.

2. Travel, while useful, is not a necessity because the cloud formations where you live are probably as elevating, and magnificent, as those found anywhere else in the world.

3. Follow the clouds, not the money.

4. Clouds are the royal road to Enlightenment: Look up at them and live.

5. Slowly move your eyes as you view the beautiful clouds against the blue green sky, near the horizon, and allow them to absorb your thoughts and mental pictures as they arise.

6. With time and practice, one should be able to view the majestic clouds continuously, while only hearing the sound of the wind, with minimal thought, for hours on end.

7. Cloud gazing, the royal road to Illumination, requires one to look deeply into the slowly changing glorious structures, the most beautiful sights in the world, for as long as one can, without thinking and without feeling anything other than joy; the longer one can comfortably concentrate, the more enlightened one has become.

9. Positive Thought

1. Although it may contradict all that we observe, it is best to believe that all is for the best, and that we are getting better and stronger everyday.

2. Affirm with absolute certainty that you will receive what you wish for, and give thanks for it; if your concentration is strong enough, it may be granted to you, for this is the prayer of faith.

3. Man, like the stock market, can talk himself up to the heights of prosperity, or down to depression.

4. Positive thought is the next best thing to Truth itself.

5. The positive thinker should believe, with absolute certainty, that if he strives for Truth, transcendence, and withdrawal from materialism through meditation, his soul will soar upon death, to perfect union with God, and he will achieve eternal life.

6. Since the center of our being is Peace and Love, and because this fact should be accepted, if only as an aspect of positive thinking, it makes no sense to read depressing books, listen to angry music, or watch violent movies.

7. News today is negative, but we must all strive to be positive; therefore, we should not listen to or watch programs about current events that merely reiterate the cliché that bad people do bad things to bad or good people, or that terrible tragedies occur in the world.

8. The way to eliminate bad thoughts is to go to the extreme opposite and eliminate all thoughts through meditation; then refill the mind with positive thoughts, no matter how illogical or impossible they may be, for these constitute the life you live when not at rest in Being.

9. Trick your child into believing she is well when she isn't, and outwit yourself in the same way as well.

10. The easiest way for a child to catch cold is for her mother to warn her about it.

11. Deny illness in yourself and your children by reiterating positive words of perfect health.

12. Because your thoughts are your life, when you are not in the Spirit, make them the best they can be, and do not linger in negativity.

13. Just say No to your doctor if he gives you a negative diagnosis, and remember that millions were healed of diseases that physicians said were incurable.

14. If the symptom appears innocuous, a merciful doctor will not needlessly worry his patient, and exacerbate the manifestation, with a discussion of worst case scenarios.

10. Love

1. Take the easy way out: Love everyone, no matter what they say or do to you.

2. Love is the sword of the soul, and the greatest defense against our fears, and the slings and arrows of others.

3. Ironically, universal Love is directly proportional to the distance between the heart and feelings, for Love cannot bloom when one unconsciously experiences reactions and emotions.

4. The ability to experience romantic love may not be a prerequisite for progress in spirituality, but it is a sign that ones defenses are not too strong, and that one is more open to the Present.

5. Although romantic love is over exaggerated in the West, it is always best, particularly in the long term, if both participants, rather than one, are capable of experiencing strong attraction to one another.

6. Money can buy neither romantic love nor Love.

7. While it is not easy, if you can help others who have hurt you, and not hold grudges, you will be part of a very small and exclusive group, which includes the greatest men and women that have ever walked the face of the earth.

11. Healing

1. The belief in the eternal life of the soul of those who achieve a certain level of being, found in early philosophy, and certain religions such as Christianity, is the best way for man to overcome the traumatic fear of death, that is one of the greatest sources of sickness on earth.

2. The panacea is the Present, and the elixir is the Now; stillness is our salvation.

3. Loneliness is the feeling that the Present, your best friend, is your enemy.

4. Good books are like crutches for the soul, but once we are healed, and the heart is opened to the greater Being around us, we no longer need them for support, and can give them to our friends and loved ones.

5. Sometimes it takes a massive blow to the ego, like an accident, illness, or shock, to provide the motive to try to scuttle the ego altogether, and seek Life on a much higher level.

6. Accidents, shocks, disenchantments, sudden loss of loved ones, and betrayals, ironically, are often the best way to break through our defenses, the buffers of the ages, and make progress in the Way.

7. If a hurtful event ultimately leads to a good result, that is often the case, remember only the good outcome, not the painful antecedent.

8. A thought is written across the mind, like a line of chalk across a blackboard, but while the eraser, or Present, can always eradicate the chalk, the chalk cannot affect the eraser.

9. One way to reduce the excessive stimulation of the heart is to observe it during meditation.

10. Nothing and no one should ever disturb the great, deep, and unfathomable Peace within.

11. Illness grounds us in unreality.

12. All ailments merit our undivided inattention.

13. Life is the stage upon which we "act out" our emotions and illnesses.

14. The physical symptom may be a part of the body that breaks down when the organism cannot contain the excitation or emotional flood that overwhelms it; the body is like a balloon filled with water that expands upon over stimulation causing a fissure in the spot that is the physical symptom.

15. We must patiently wait as the symptom is alleviated, often after a long period, when excitation is reduced, or when the body acclimates to a higher level of stimulation.

16. The false manifestation of illness that appears and feels all too real may appear when ego fear constricts the flow of blood to a particular part of the body.

17. In order to understand that illness is largely cause by stress, try to remember the number of times you went to the doctor with a symptom that was sub clinical, or false.

18. Healing involves divesting the mind from attending to that part of the body that is imperfect, by realizing that the kingdom of God is within, and that it is not we who live, but God who lives in us.

19. We are always being healed by the indwelling of the Holy Spirit.

20. Believe you are healed unto death.

21. The big lie of sickness is the idea that one will always remain ill, and no matter how many times one recovers, one still mistakenly believes one will never get better.

22. Illnesses are psychological shell games in the sense that they are interchangeable, for when one gets a new one, the old one is forgotten, recedes into insignificance, as it is healed by Mind.

23 It is fine to discuss your problems with friends, but not to excess; difficulties should be meditated away, rather than talked out, because Truth and silence, rather than words, are curative.

24. The ego does not understand Truth, and is traumatized by being injured by another ego, but being hurt does not confer sin upon the victim, nor prevent the quest for Peace, and is therefore an irrelevant occurrence.

25. Sleep more and drive slowly.

26. An illness immediately causes a distemper of negative thoughts about its causes, and how the sickness should have been avoided; if you work backwards, and eliminate the negative thoughts through meditation, the ailment is alleviated.

27. A slight congenital circulatory disability, which is quite common, and the cause of much negative thought, cannot be alleviated by stimulating psychotherapeutic dialogue, but can be relieved by deeper levels of rest through meditation.

28. As we strive for higher levels of spirituality, the body may

develop a sub-clinical physical symptom, that modern medicine cannot diagnose, that is merely God's way of telling us that we must still live in the body, to a certain degree, while on earth.

29. Illness is bad enough, but the diagnosis is the real killer.

30. Better to be hooked on vitamins and food supplements than prescription drugs.

31. The suffering of most people, derived from injury at the hands of others, leads to over excitation of the mind and body; the only way to reduce over stimulation is to go to the other extreme of deep rest in the Present, without the added agitation of the past or future.

32. The only way to overcome the residual pain from a trauma caused by someone is to avoid the observation or mental visualization of that person.

33. God helps those who see themselves, or heals those who remember Him.

34. We are always being regenerated, and the death is merely the point at which we run out of the energy required to complete the recovery.

35. Medical commercials that discuss disease, surgery, prescriptions, and hospitalization implant fear and negativity in the mind, and are thus highly undesirable for the seeker.

36. Medical advertising reminds us of diseases we may have or have had, and are very harmful because healing occurs when illness is forgotten, not remembered.

37. The medical and prescription drug industries perpetuate fear, which is precisely the opposite of what is required for a speedy recovery, and people may be frightened to death by

their often unfounded suggestions.

38. Weak, incompetent, greedy, or unscrupulous doctors often prescribe unnecessary and invasive medical solutions for purely psychosomatic symptoms.

39. Rather than see a doctor, it is often better to visit a nutritionist, and take good quality vitamin and food supplements, as symptoms frequently disappear as the body becomes stronger.

40. Western medicine has a limited repertoire of solutions to health problems, and many surgeries may be avoided if people broaden their horizons with herbal, homeopathic, Eastern, and nutritional forms of healing and preventive medicine.

41. Peace is a better physician than prayer.

42. High blood pressure, one of the greatest killers in society today, is proof of the need to seek Peace, and is one of the greatest sources of motivation for the Eternal Quest.

43. God's purpose in trauma or tragedy is to demonstrate to the sufferer the power of negative thought, and to neutralize it; redemption, the greatest prize that man can achieve, is much more difficult without the motivation that suffering provides.

44. Drink decaffeinated green tea and take fish oil supplements.

45. To accelerate your healing, spend more time in the Spirit.

46. Evil and insanity result from the misconception that the Present is tormenting rather than tranquil.

47. Sin is a primary cause of sickness because falseness is arduous.

48. Let go and let God or the Now, heal you.

49. The expression, "Physician, heal thyself," is true in the sense that a person cannot heal another unless he can feel the presence of God within, and then channel it to the sufferer, with or without the laying on of hands.

50. In the West, healing is achieved through the bracing, and distracting quest for meaning in work or creativity, and in the East, wholeness is gained through tranquility; the latter is superior because it is more effective, less agitating, and open to all, not just the employed, energetic, or most talented in society.

51. The wisest among the enlightened have suffered a lot and those who have not had ego or health problems, that had to be overcome, are usually of less help to the seeker; most of the greatest healers were traumatized at some point in their lives.

52. Rather than a barrage of words, often insensitively spoken, simple love and support from friends is always good medicine, in times of trouble.

53. The mentally ill person can only be assisted if he can be convinced that what he imagines is true is actually false.

54. The Spirit in us is not diminished by the traumatic loss of any kind of external loved object, because Spirit is non-physical, and separate or distinct from concrete negative thought forms; many have been healed of serious diseases by the existential understanding and acceptance of this simple fact.

12. Objective and Subjective Truth

1. A person who does not believe in objective standards of truth is like a blind man who cannot understand why he is unable to see, or why those with vision move around so easily.

2. Those who believe values are subjective engage in far more psychological lying in defense of the ego than those who subscribe to universal standards of objective truth.

3. The idea that one should live for others is a consequence of the belief in objective truth; the doctrine of self-interest results from allegiance to subjective or personal values.

4. Two negative results of the weakening of virtue and standards of objectivity in the societal revolution of the 1960's are the lionization of criminality, and the development of the false biography, in literature and film.

5. Youth entering most college today are brainwashed into believing in subjectivism, or cultural relativism; this personal, idiosyncratic theory of truth is reflected in the absurd notion that one man's terrorist is another's freedom fighter, or that reality is always in the eye of the beholder.

6. In order to truly progress in the Way, one must realize that cannibalism is not a mode of cognition or value system that is as valid as Christianity.

7. Standards of absolute truth are essential as a yardstick for moral behavior, and the opposite, or moral relativism, which is the notion that good and evil are indistinguishable, cannot be accepted by the true seeker, who should always be found near church or temple.

13. Teachers

1. Great teachers gain fame from their exalted and humble students, posthumously.

2. The acknowledgement of the teacher by the student increases rather than decreases the authority or notoriety of the student, and Plato was enlarged by his enormous tribute to Socrates.

3. It is highly unlikely that a person, under the common order of emotions, can have understanding without the divine intervention of a teacher, who knows the Truth.

4. The greatest unanswered question in your life is not, "Will I find the right woman, profession, or creative vocation of my dreams?", but, "Will I meet a great teacher, and be open to his or her good influence, and raise my level of being to help others become better people?"

5. A great teacher will give you great memories, but most of those reminiscences will be non-specific, without external referents, because you both imbibed in the greater Being of the universe.

6. The bible in and of itself is not a teacher, for many ignorant people carry it with them all the time; a teacher is a person who had a good teacher who embodied the bible, and was willing to transmit his or her knowledge and understanding to a humble, inquisitive, respectful, and ultimately obedient student.

7. A wise person is someone who merely puts a little twist on the great understanding of his teacher, who also deserves little

credit for having only been a vessel of his or her teacher's knowledge.

8. Teachers whose teachers were post-modernist, or cut off from the great chain of morality that under girds the major religions, are limited in that they can only advocate transcendentalism, garnished by a few examples, here and there, of noble behavior, that are insufficient to eliminate falseness, and understand Truth.

9. You may never find a great individual teacher to implant the importance of virtue, and release you from sensation, but the church is a good teacher, and the best mentor that is available to most people in western society today.

10. Some children have superb, slightly excessive being, accompanied by poor concentration, and must take special education courses, or be taken to child psychologists; ironically, many of these kids have great spiritual potential if, by God's grace, they find the right teacher in church, temple, or everyday life.

14. Materialism, Sensation, & Over Stimulation

1. Life is sensational when not in sensation.

2. Materialism does not only refer to an involvement with physical objects, but also the investment of psychic energy in mental constructs and pictures, or anything that is not pure Spirit.

3. Most seek sensation and as a consequence do not achieve sensibility; one achieves sensibility and becomes sensible only by withdrawing from sensation.

4. Success cannot be measured with a ruler or adding machine.

5. Accept no cheap materialist substitutes: Move into the glory of God and stay there.

6. A man's obsession with electronics and machinery, including automobiles, is one of the greatest impediments to spirituality.

7. Some are so filled with thoughts, opinions, and emotions that one cannot sit with them for more than a few minutes without experiencing over stimulation, so far removed are these unfortunate people from the Peace of God.

8. Excellence in materialism, or facility in technical, and professional matters, leads to "success", but is always unconscious and unsatisfying, and of limited value and importance.

9. Expensive jewelry is attractive, but unnecessarily stimulating; if lost or marred, great disturbance results, and we should not put our selves in such a vulnerable position.

10. Do not wear a cell phone on your ear.

11. No one willfully wants to be a perpetual motion machine.

12. Many accidents involving physical injury occur as we unconsciously rush through life, trying to complete our chores as soon as possible; they can be avoided only by slowing down.

13. Invest in God and divest from sensation, and, ironically, the material world is gained thereby.

14. Ethnocentrism, or racism, is the apotheosis of materialism, because ethnicity and skin pigmentation are physical quantities.

15. The expression, "A penny for your thoughts," is based upon the fact that this is about all they are worth.

16. Thoughts are subtle, almost invisible, like a chameleon blending into the tree of being, but if we are still enough, we can see them, and not be governed by them, but by the greater Being around us.

17. Mysticism posits that the pause between actions should be increased because it is a source of greater happiness than thoughts, images, feelings, or movements.

18. He who has little time, or is overly concerned about wasting it, is moving too fast, and accomplishes little, spiritually.

19. As nice as a conversation may be, it is always a bit of a letdown for the seeker who has made progress in the Divine Science.

20. Materialism is singling out an aspect of a person, not related to his values, and judging based upon that characteristic.

21. Because it is a reaction to a mere false accusation, that is unrelated to Reality or morality, anger toward others for a misjudgment about oneself is sheer materialism.

22. Most people can only see the surface of things today because they live totally materialist lives; understanding involves abstraction that may not be accompanied by concrete referents that have length, width, and breadth.

23. Sense the reality of the greater Being that surrounds you and be set free of the world of sensation and reaction, and as you create a larger space in your consciousness, you will limit the activities of your reactive mind.

24. A person is blocked, and borders on insanity, if he is stuck in excessive sensation, full of fears and arrogance, and cannot even see Reality for a mere moment.

25. Man's thought raises him above other animals, but, ironically, if thinking is not reduced, he remains on the animal level.

26. Most over achievers have, ironically, asked far too little of themselves in life, being content with merely continuing, refining, and expanding upon the same concatenation of reactions and sensations inherited from their parents and society.

27. The mystic does not believe in creativity unless he is building a bigger soul, or higher being, with which to meet God.

28. Many artists, poets, musicians, and writers are deeply materialist, seeped in thoughts, mental pictures, and objects,

and envious of the mystic, because they know that the spiritual seeker is onto something important, that they can never understand, or reach, without the kind of effort that would take them away from their work.

29. The artist always strives to achieve the perfect object and does not wish for this effort to ever end, but the mystic strives to end all endeavors by attaining the perfection of his own self through unity with the infinite.

30. The problem with reading is that your head is facing down when it should be turned upward.

31. All material objects deemed valuable by society have no redeeming metaphysical value.

32. Snub your nose at the Present by relentlessly remaining in sensation and action at your own peril.

33. Words and thoughts are expendable; the space around them is essential.

34. Sadly, the vast majority of the world will only stop moving, talking, thinking, feeling, imagining, and dreaming when they die.

35. It is lamentable that the precocious, or those of very high intelligence, are in the unenviable position of needing much sensation to satiate their souls; similarly, even the intelligent have problems freeing themselves from a life of excessive mental stimulation that is an escape from Reality, or the Present moment.

36. Political talk radio is over stimulating and contrary to spirituality.

37. Movies are a good source for observing strong emotional reactions, or things one should avoid in real life.

38. A sign of spiritual progress is increased sensitivity, and the inability to tolerate graphic violence in movies and other media.

39. The problem with consumerism and excessive materialism is that we tend to worry too much about unnecessary objects that may get damaged, scratched, or broken, and these concerns further attach us to the material world.

40. Physical beauty may be a spiritual handicap because the increase in superficial personal power, vanity, and desirability disturb the beautiful seeker's consciousness, and put her at a disadvantage when compared to her less attractive friends.

41. Learn not to talk to your lover or spouse for prolonged periods, as conversation and reactions are not necessities of life, and improve your relationship dramatically.

42. The life of sensation was most forcefully advocated and defended in the stories of Hemmingway: wine, women, hunting in Africa, bullfights in Spain, and lifelong regret for the loss of a woman whose image eternally lingers in the mind.

43. We cannot see the forest of Being, for the trees, or things, around us.

44. Bread may be the staff of small "l" life, but not Life because it has breadth.

45. The purpose of understanding why people react as they do is to avoid reacting to their reactions.

46. Meticulousness, or a type of nervousness that is caused by the fear of unpleasant feelings if a certain object of material value is damaged, is the bane of the highly sensitive seeker, for it chains him to the material world, from which he is trying to escape.

47. Modern movies, stimulants, alcohol, news reports, newspapers, medical and hospital advertisements with their suggestions of illness, prescription drug commercials, fast highway driving, excessive, unnecessary reading, competitive sports, and crazy identification with athletes or favorite teams, foster materialism and are contrary to the Eternal Quest.

48. People who need to be fulfilled by material objects, or power, fame, and the presence of others do not recognize that they are not empty, but full, if they could only meditate until Reality becomes known.

49. Because of the materialist nature of unethical behavior, one must question the spirituality of an amoral or immoral person.

50. There is no devil worth mentioning because he is merely the personification of negativity or materialism, and as such should not exist.

51. Ironically, the psychotherapist, or "shrink", adds words and thoughts to the neurotic's mind or ego that has already been enlarged by them.

52. Those with poor being are often somewhat inert, and in constant need of stimulation and companionship to combat loneliness; they should try to fight unpleasant feelings of isolation by quietly sitting alone, without excitation, for longer periods.

53. All of life's stresses, struggles, and emotions, including marital conflict, children's rebellion, jealousy, anger, and fear are solely reactions to externals, whose solution lies in withdrawal from the physical for solace and Peace in the spiritual.

54. If someone treats you badly, take it as a cue to look up and live, rather than stay down and react on the material level.

55. The more disturbed a person becomes, the more he is in need of sensation to block out the beloved Present, that sadly feels so intolerable.

56. Compulsive conversationalists, or those in need of higher levels of sensation to subdue pain and frustration, must sit still, take a mild tranquilizer for a little while, and begin to meditate, until the pain in the chest begins to subside, and they can live alone in comfort.

57. Radio and television psychotherapists are of limited value because they are unaware of Reality, and prefer to heal only with words, or materialist methods.

58. Reduced spending is always beneficial because it reduces excitation; excessive spending fully illustrates the bottomless pit of the life of sensation that is empty, and never truly satisfying.

59. Anything is too expensive, if one does not need it; do not enter stores unless you are in need of something, as the desire for material things should not be unnecessarily intensified.

60. The excessive levels of sensation and stimulation that our children are exposed to in movies and media may make them more easily bored, and less likely to ever have the patience to stop, and achieve Wisdom.

15. Imagination, Mental Pictures, & Negative Thought

1. A picture is worth a thousand words, which is why imagination is more potent, and potentially more harmful, than thought.

2. Thought is a finite thing that is limited in time and space; space is infinite, and will always dominate the finite, if one will let it.

3. The greatest achievement a man or woman can have in life is to erase a repetitive negative image from memory.

4. Nothing bad or painful is worth thinking about, even for a second.

5. Pathos is a passion for the past, not the Present.

6. Craziness usually results from life in the waking dream state of thought, feeling, and pictures, or imagination, not the meditative state of Life.

7. The only way to conquer what is called in religious parlance the devil, or negative thought, is through the Peace of God.

8. Deposit your negative thoughts and mental pictures in a cloud bank and watch them disappear.

9. Ironically, people with good being or innate simple self-awareness, as opposed to excessive worry, imagination, and negative thought, are less likely to move to Peace and Wisdom because they are self–satisfied; those blessed with poor being are more likely to make the great leap forward to a higher level, because they are strongly motivated by the

desire to feel better.

10. Memories, or aspects of imagination or physical quantities lingering in the mind, have been lionized, of late, in the media and movies in the West; they are best forgotten, as they reduce time spent more usefully in the blissful Present.

11. Although they are generally less harmful, some who write a lot of books often suffer from a similar form of madness as those who hoard a lot of money: excessive imagination and excitation about how many people are reading one's writings before or after one dies, or how many things one can buy with one's riches.

12. The most enlightened spread Love to those around them, and teach by example, but generally do not write books, because they are no longer at the mercy of their imagination, or pictures of themselves being admired by others; they also have no need to be included in the historical record.

13. The small ego mind is very opportunistic as it scavenges for something negative to focus upon; this further exemplifies the importance and urgency of moving up and out of sensation to higher spiritual levels.

14. To be in a good space is to create a space within; to be in a bad space is to have a mind that is always cluttered, such that the space in the center cannot be known.

15. Freud, the father of modern psychology, was so completely wrapped up in his interminable words, thoughts, and imagination that he could not see that the happiness we all seek is not in ideas and mental pictures.

16. We exist in a deep sea of Being, and should ignore the flotsam and jetsam of thoughts and feelings that reside on the surface.

17. There is a tendency to tarry over negative thoughts and pictures and repeat them, but we must block them out immediately, and focus upon God within and without.

18. The mind is like a haunted house with ghosts of the past or bad memories, in every closet; allow meditation or the Now to close the closet doors as soon as they open, until they remain closed forever.

19. The only way for a person to avoid being a masochistic memory machine is to step into the Present.

20. Do not let yourself be governed by any physical quantities floating through the mind, particularly in the form of painful pictures of people you knew in the past.

21. The purpose of a negative thought is to remind us of God.

22. We are defeated only if we think about evil, bad people, or those who have hurt us.

23. A thought is like a page turning in the book called mind; choose the one you want, or close the book.

24. If a negative thought comes your way, snap out of it, and then let the Present remove it from your consciousness.

25. If a negative thought or picture is entertained for ten seconds, bring in the Present moment for twenty seconds, and increase dosages of the Now, proportionately, as required; thus one can prove to oneself, and others, the predominance of the Present.

26. As soon as a negative thought rears its ugly head, shoot it down with the Present moment; let the Now do your dirty work, for negativity, like the devil, cannot stand up to the Now, or God, for a nanosecond.

27. Negative thoughts and pictures should be merely observed,

like a bird flying by, but not entertained or indulged, even for one moment, if possible.

28. If you feel sad, depressed, or angry, do not rehash the negativity, but look up, and move to the high plateau, above the plain, or pain, of human existence.

29. Most people do not appreciate the power of imagination until a traumatic image, caused by sorrow or hatred, that is difficult to dislodge except through meditation, gets stuck in the mind, and causes "dis ease".

30. A picture in the mind is worth a thousand thoughts; this fact signifies that a trauma is an indelible image, rather than a thought, that embeds in the mind, to be eventually neutralized by meditation.

31. Cervantes's great novel, "Don Quixote", is about a lunatic who cared only for the high he experienced after his imagined acts of benevolence that were, in reality, so harmful to himself and others; confusion or psychopathology occurs when someone imagines he is a great humanitarian, but cannot see that he only cares about himself, not others.

16. Arrogance

1. Unfortunately, the most intelligent generally do not understand the important things in life because they think they know everything, are self-important, and not open to proper guidance from the right teacher, that requires humility.

2. Those that are always right in their own minds, or can never admit mistakes, will never learn anything of importance in life.

3. Pretense or pretension is a form of arrogance perfectly exhibited in people who pretend to have expertise in all things, but have little knowledge of any of the fields that they claim to understand.

4. As King Solomon will attest, too much knowledge is a terrible thing in the sense that it is usually accompanied by the immovable bedrock of vanity.

5. The personal pride of the small ego in its achievements is acceptable, but self-flattery, or the obsessive concern about how good one is for doing different things, is not beneficial.

6. Avoid the self-flattery of excessive speech, or the pleasure of listening to yourself as you speak to others.

7. If success entails even a slight increase in arrogance, choose professional mediocrity.

8. Curtailing criticism, an aspect of arrogance that involves looking down upon others, is critical.

9. Criticism is never good for the faultfinder, but can be a useful tonic to increase self-restraint or non-reaction in the recipient.

10. Mental disorder is a form of hubris that prevents one from seeing that one has a problem; once one is humble enough to know that one is not well, one can be redeemed.

11. The gratuitous lies of the arrogant are not free but come at a great price: the inability to ever know the Truth that sets one free.

17. Envy

1. There is nothing to envy in someone who is solely in imagination, unless he is a moral person.

2. Only envy another if he has greater access to the Now, or is more other directed than you, for all else is immaterial materialism.

3. Envious people are jealous of others for their money, wives, husbands and other material things, but their greatest opprobrium is often reserved for those who have achieved a higher level of being.

4. There is no point in envying another for his material goods, because one never knows if that person is on a high level of being or consciousness that is far more important than possessions.

18. Regret

1. One should never regret not knowing someone, visiting somewhere, or having something; one should only miss the Spirit when one is not aware of it.

2. Rather than regret a few errors along the way, we must be eternally grateful for the privilege of being born a human being, the highest form of life in the known universe.

3. Regret is a total misperception of Reality, for it is the belief that the mere loss of an object, rather than the lack of contact with Being, is a catastrophe.

4. We are here for a nanosecond, through no effort of our own, yet all the while we wring our hands about how things could have been so much better had we not made certain decisions in the past.

5. Life is a series of trade offs in which we get vanilla but lose chocolate; our error is the belief that we can have both vanilla and chocolate in our extremely short time on earth.

6. A regretful memory should remind us of Mind.

7. Regret results from the illogical belief that a bad decision which results in a little suffering but ultimately leads to a good conclusion should still be reversed.

8. The wise do not say, "If only I had made that other decision, I could have been a happy person," but count their blessings, no matter how small, every day.

19. Flattery

1. The sleaziness of the flatterer cannot be detected by people who do not have good values, and this fact further demonstrates the need for moral development and progress in virtue.

2. The phrase, "Flattery will get you nowhere," is true in more ways than one, as one cannot begin the great walk to Truth, if one still suffers from the malady of false behavior, in the service of the base.

3. While on the surface he handles her with kindness, a flatterer is a man who treats a woman as a sex object.

4. Many women with low self-esteem and poor guidance flatter themselves into believing they are good for being liked by a male flatterer.

5. While ultimately everyone should be forgiven by the belief in the universal love of God and man, without a concept of absolute truth from which to measure behavior in the material world, the flatterer cannot be distinguished from the true friend, good cannot be distinguished from evil, nor truth from falsehood, and chaos results.

6. The flatterer may be distinguished by the fact that he places no value upon values, and is thus incapable of generous acts of love, kindness, or forgiveness, unless he has an ulterior motive, such as a desire for fame, power, money, or sex.

20. Anger

1. Although sensitive, the more highly evolved are less likely to be hurt by another's words.

2. The inflated ego is easily deflated by one wrong word; one may not speak freely with the egoist who needs continuous stroking to prevent hostility from erupting.

3. The paranoiac feels you are critical of him when you are kind; our goal is the obverse: to be kind to those who actually are critical of us.

4. Work, while important, should not be a defense mechanism against poor being or ego pain that one does not wish to acknowledge or overcome.

5. Try not to get too angry with your child solely for exhibiting certain aspects of your character.

6. Just because a person looks unattractive is no reason for him to spend a life in anger; if his frustration can be overcome through meditation, he will soar way above the so-called beautiful people, who may be ugly inside, and have no interest in Truth, which are both far more serious maladies than the inability to obtain certain material pleasures.

7. The best reply to unimportant criticism, that occurs most of the time, is silence, until the anger subsides, as reactions often make matters worse.

8. Anger is a form of ignorance that results from the belief that everyone on the level of ego is truthful, wise, and good; the belief in the evil nature of ego obviates the need for anger.

9. An argument may be the folly that one can raise the level of understanding of another person in a short span of time, or the outcome of the false belief that another person knows as much as you, but pretends otherwise.

10. The most unfortunate are the disobedient, or those who feel alive only when in conflict, rather than at peace with others; they are born stubborn and restless, and rebel against others first, but blame them for starting the dispute.

11. One is relieved of righteous indignation with the realization that the corruption of world values is the inevitable result of the pure necessity, or prior causation that can only be reversed by the grace of God.

12. Anger is the admission that one could not find the cause of another's criticism in time to prevent one's reaction.

13. Men should reign in their hostility from improper upbringing, or genetic predisposition, rather than spend a lifetime acting out a life of pure necessity, with no progress in virtue or spirituality.

14. Anger is an inference, or thought, that occurs immediately after someone disrespects you or expresses anger towards you in words; we should try not to make any inferences, as we might have been insensitive toward the other first, and just allow the angry feeling, that is not unpleasant in itself, to pass.

15. Anger often stems from the perceived need to correct a person's misunderstanding of ourselves, and to convince that person of his error; but this is one area in which ego reaction is not required; rather, it is often best to let the aggrieved maintain his own perception of things, and hope that all can let go, and move forward into Life, without the need to enhance the ego, or false self, by retaliation.

16. It is unfair to say, "My father abused me, so I abuse my child. Don't blame me, blame my father"; unfortunately, many people do not take responsibility for their actions, or cannot see their insensitivity toward the child as the primary cause of the child's rebelliousness.

17. The present rage within us from the suffering of our ancestors causes us to perceive evil motives in others, when such is not the case; only be meditating out the pain can we be redeemed from the incapacity to see the facts of our lives.

18. Aggressive drivers have a long way to go before they can slow down, no less stop their activities, on the road to Enlightenment.

19. Repress anger: Never use words such as idiot, jerk, retarded, bastard, bitch, or any obscenities.

21. Boredom

1. Boredom is the inactive, unobserved self that cannot contemplate Being during the space between activities.

2. Boredom is the unobserved, unconscious ego searching space for substance, not knowing that space itself is substantial; it is the false feeling that the bliss of Being is frustrating.

3. Bored people do not realize that the source of their unease is the Present, or Life everlasting, and although it will be very difficult at first, they need to stop and meditate, until their frustration is alleviated, and the Now becomes a beloved friend, not an enemy.

22. Fame & Power

1. One can never achieve Enlightenment if one's gurus were one's college teachers in the '60's, and one's mantra is, "Seek power, fame, sex, and money, for life is meaningless."

2. Be generous and forgiving to those who are solely in imagination and have little interest in seeking Truth, for all they may ever obtain, through paltry contrivances, are fame, power, money, and sex.

3. Governed by love of fame, many Western idealist and existentialist philosophers did not ask us to cultivate intuition, but attempted to explain the simple concept of Being, Spirit, or the non-material space around us in a most pretentious, complicated, and unreadable fashion.

4. A form of love of fame is the pleasurable highs we get from knowing, or being near, rich, famous, or important people; seekers should try to overcome this common tendency of natural man.

5. The worst thing about attaining power or fame is that one becomes type caste, and must spend most of one's time working against type, in order to live in Life or Truth.

6. Power and fame have nothing to do with real supremacy, mastery, and authority; to the contrary, dominion and notoriety in the natural world are normally inversely related to the greater goods in life.

7. Those who seek worldly power, fame, or money allow themselves to be governed by their own imagination, but true existential power resides in the Spirit, and is not contingent

upon our fluctuating mental pictures and thoughts, or the action of others.

8. Man gains real power with the increased availability and predominance of the Now in his life, not through formal or social power over others, in work or society.

9. Because it impedes the development of a spiritual life, the quest for political power and fame, accompanied by mental pictures of public adulation and admiration, is childish and fruitless.

23. Sex

1. In this promiscuous world, it is hard for young men and women to find partners for satisfying lifelong relationships.

2. Excessive sexual stimulation leads to the over aggressiveness of men toward women; couples should never lose sight of the negative effects of unnatural, immoderate sensuality, such as the need for greater levels of sensation, and the loss of Being awareness, caused by vivid, repetitive imagination, that gets stronger every day.

3. A belief in abstinence is rightly enhanced by the recognition of the risks of pregnancy in or out of marriage, and sexually transmitted disease.

4. Members of this generation X can only develop a spiritual life, or true Wisdom, if they first realize that there is more to life than sex; if they concentrate solely upon one another for meaning, they will remain cynically mired in sensation and materialism, and can never extricate themselves from external dependencies.

5. The problem with the excessive sexuality is that one can never move beyond the finitude of various partners, who totally dominate consciousness, and the increased dependency upon externals, that result in increased imagination, yearning, and other undesirable emotions.

6. Some men get a feeling of self enhancement by having sex with as many women as possible, but this will never compensate for the lack of real contact with the natural, no less supernatural, worlds.

7. On the level of nature, sex is relevant, as it is among the great apes, but on the level above nature, it is not significant; if sex was as important as psychologists contend, it would not be an activity shared by monkeys.

24. Greed

1. Break the wall between your being, or soul, and the greater Being around you; money is of no use in this effort, and cannot satisfy your being if it is encased in the hard, almost impenetrable, shell of the ego.

2. Money, while important for necessities and security, is the root of materialism and imagination, and gives a false sense of empowerment, because it does not reduce sensation, or increase being, but only increases one's potential to buy more objects that are impediments to spirituality.

3. Wealth is normally accompanied by the fear of loss of money, a sense of superiority, imperiousness, and an unhealthy disregard for others that is disguised by flattery.

4. Love of money, like egoic love for another person, chains one to the object world from which one must separate, in order to have greater awareness of the Being that pervades the universe.

5. The sales profession is difficult because greedy people continuously take advantage of the more ethical in the organization; it is not immoral, and should cause no guilt, if the aggrieved responds in kind, in this special situation, from time to time.

6. The amoral life of today is one of confusion, inconsistency, and contradiction, because money is not the greatest source of happiness, and is incapable of stopping the machine, even for one moment.

7. Money is counterfeit because it cannot be redeemed for Truth.

8. Money is not the currency with which we may overcome the slights of others.

9. Greed is desire run amok, and mitigates toward the belief that one should perhaps strive to eliminate desire altogether.

10. Greedy people imagine they are successful, but cannot fathom why their friends are so crass, vindictive, faultfinding, and uninteresting; the wise and morally upright are the most charming people, but have little interest in learning about the importance of money, and why it is sacred.

11. Amoral or greedy people fail as parents because they have no moral authority, and are contradictory when disciplining their children; their children perpetuate this misfortune by living a restricted, and above all confused life because on some level they do not believe that money is the greatest good.

12. The elderly greedy are generally beyond hope because their false selves are hardened, and the wise cannot break through the buffers, blockages, and defense mechanisms that form a cataract over the eyes, the windows of the soul.

13. Greediness, the cause of many family problems, is synonymous with meanness, but no one would consciously wish to be nasty, if he could avoid it.

25. Morals & Values

1. Never compare yourself to others, except with regard to progress in virtue and growth of being into Being.

2. Man needs morality more than identity; his morality molds his identity.

3. The bad are not helped by a strong sense of identity, and the good do not need it because they attain it through altruism.

4. Confusion is when one contradicts oneself within a span of ten sentences, without knowing it; it usually results from insufficient virtue, humility, and self observation.

5. People who contradict themselves, whose behavior and words are opposite, who complain about bad situations that they have caused, or who are bellicose and love to argue, are sadly confused, and must begin to see their bewilderment before spiritual progress, that requires utmost sincerity, can begin.

6. Sleaziness slays stillness through over stimulation; immorality immolates the Now.

7. If someone correctly criticizes you for your lack of good values, you should listen, and take it to heart; if the criticism is unrelated to ethics, there is no need to react, because it is simply a factual matter, and not worth excessive pother.

8. The capacity for shame is superior to fame.

9. People who own large Sports Utility Vehicles, and display disregard for endangered people in smaller cars, as well as the planet earth, set poor examples of ego control for their children.

10. People who do not pick up after their dogs are uncivilized, and almost incurably lost in materialism, from which there is probably no escape, because false self enhancement is continuously at the expense of others.

11. The amoral person, who professes to believe in virtue, but does not value goodness, and believes that the end, or so-called "success", justifies the means, is again dishonest when he criticizes another for violating the norms of conduct that he himself does not accept; this represents the fundamental fallacy of purely rationalist secular humanism.

12. Some creative people mistakenly equate creativity with piety or righteousness; the talent of invention confers no right to treat others badly, or to be absolved from the same standards as others.

13. Morality sanctifies the Holy Science.

14. Good values sustain, complete, and seal your transcendence; spirituality without morality is frivolity.

15. It is better to have integrity without spirituality, than an amoral or corruptible achievement of transcendence that is nothing more than a spiritual high.

16. The only uncorrupted area of materialism, or valid area of cognition, is morality.

17. Morality contradicts the non-conceptual nature of Reality, yet it is abstract and essential, ironically, to the final fulfillment spirituality in Enlightenment.

18. Objectivity is not possible without morality, because defending one's ego never leads to thought clarity, but only confusion, in the material world.

19. A hatred for religion does not obviate, but necessitates, a greater interest in, and avowal of, morality.

20. Immorality grounds us in materialism, and thus detracts us from spirituality.

21. The game of life is an adventure in virtue, and those who become the ethical elite, or moral millionaires, are the only winners.

22. Despite many people's belief to the contrary, a good looking person is not necessarily good.

23. The most impoverished are not the poor, or the spiritually unenlightened, but the morally bankrupt.

24. If a woman can rear her children with greater virtue without a bad husband, even in greater poverty, divorce is justifiable, because minds commingle, and the bad generally dominates the good, over time.

25. Being ideally intensifies virtue, and a vessel of Spirit or Truth should not do anything immoral, even if not trained in virtue.

26. Nice people bear grudges and reply in kind to unkindness; good people forgive and forget.

27. A simple, "Thank you', means so much and is so important, yet many cannot bring themselves around to saying these two simple words.

28. An apology is very important, and those who feel all apologies are irrelevant, or in bad faith, are to be pitied, and may have difficulties in simple human relations.

29. Be gracious, high-minded, refined, patrician, and civilized, and try to avoid criticism, that does not do anyone any good, and is a tell-tale sign of a lack of spiritual and moral

development.

30. While laudable and a sign of caring, the need to be near the family does not confer rectitude, nor obviate the need for progress in virtue.

31. A certain degree of credit should be given to those who try, but fail, to morally improve themselves significantly, as they are on a higher level of life than those who do not try at all.

32. The real philosopher is the good person.

33. Bad people, or those who harm the innocent without reason, should be loved, because they may be without hope of redemption.

34. The bad can only teach us how not to behave if they can be distinguished from the good.

35. Many great old novels are educational because they taught how to distinguish injurious from good people when the iniquitous, through flattery, appeared honorable on the surface.

36. Nice guys would not finish last, but first, if they were good.

37. The wise feel pity for those who are either slightly dishonest or completely corrupt, but the ignorant will unreservedly confide in the former, and only mildly disapprove of the latter.

38. Some New Thought philosophers are too politically correct to take morality seriously.

39. Sadly, a friend today may be defined as someone who sides with you when you are in a dispute with another person, and are at fault.

40. Most people flatter themselves into believing they are

good when they are not even nice; it would take many years for them to begin to achieve any real goodness or virtue and a loving countenance.

41. Anyone who strives to be good is a success.

42. Most college teachers learned little of ethical importance from their instructors and thus have little to offer you; unless university educators learned something of moral importance from their mentors, they will have little, beyond the level of technical information, to offer you.

43. Secular college education today is risky because while it is correlated with an increase in technical or professional knowledge, it may result in a diminution of moral literacy.

44. If you know you have a tendency to be somewhat dishonest or sleazy, get a salaried job, and try to overcome your disability, rather than a job in sales, as too many people go into professions that enhance, rather than reduce, moral weakness.

45. Have high-minded friends that continuously whisper in your ear, "Be good and do the right thing," for they are the most important influences in your life.

46. Psychological lying, in which parents teach their children to be defense attorneys for their every word and action, to blame others for their own mistakes, or to deny many things that they have actually said and done, is sadly rampant today, in traditional and secular societies.

47. Bad people are arrogant and irrational because they take other people for the fools that they themselves are, without knowing it.

48. Most people's standard of rectitude is so low that even God cannot find and help them.

49. Intelligence without spiritual and moral development is meaningless.

50. Values refer to personal ethics, not political opinions; people who do not have good character believe that values are an aspect of politics.

51. Some people say, "He is a nice guy, but he borrowed $10,000 from his friend, and did not return it," but, to avoid confusion, our standards of virtue should be a little higher, as we define a dishonest person as immoral.

52. Corporations often have low integrity at the top because owners and CEO's are surrounded by flatterers out to destroy others who may threaten their position in the pecking order; thus many painful and often traumatic dismissals or firings have no validity at all, since they are based upon partial, inadequate information, and lies, motivated by revenge and petty maliciousness on the part of inhuman, power mad people who will stop at nothing to achieve their ends.

53. As one grows in being and values, one's standards become higher, corruption and criminality are more easily discerned, and one is less likely to define deviancy down, or consent to immorality in oneself and others.

54. One's ability to see the perfunctory, but not insignificant, evil in others is moral discernment that is only possible in those who are aware of their own lack of virtue; however, on a deeper level, one should strive to love everyone, and see the goodness at the core of the soul, beneath the ego.

55. If you wish to understand a person's character, ask him who were the most important influences in his life, and why they were significant.

56. Even if insufficiently enhanced by their mothers, manly men will not spend their lives seeking self-enhancement at the

expense of women.

57. Before one can be moral, one must be polite.

58. While one should not be hypercritical, one must be able to recognize the degree of virtue in others, and by seeing their ethical insufficiencies, as well as one's own, all can evolve together; if bad people are believed to be good merely because of a few good actions, that is more often the case, ethical confusion results, and no progress in virtue for oneself, or others, is possible.

59. It is comical when the moral relativist bases his judgments on anything but morality because this makes him utterly incapable of understanding his own or other people's behavior.

26. Conscience

1. The paradox of conscience is that some people have more, and others less, yet it is a non-material compartment of the soul, or aspect of being; if, through nature or nurture, it is undeveloped, it must be rebuilt by family, noble people, church, or temple.

2. The greatest mistake of modern psychology and the '60's generation is the attempted destruction of the superego or conscience, just because some uninformed parents were overly oppressive with their children.

3. A lack of conscience means that if you can get something beneficial for yourself, at the expense of another, without the possibility of being caught, you will take advantage of the situation; true Wisdom is not possible under these circumstances.

4. If today's New Thought metaphysician believes that one can take a person, who does not believe in conscience at all, and teach him to meditate his way to Truth, he is sadly mistaken, for true Enlightenment is made of sterner stuff.

5. Modern psychology does not understand that guilt about the violation of eternal moral verities is wellness, not infirmity.

27. Woman

1. Women must learn that there is no need to rationalize thoughts and actions that are merely aspects of ego or materialism, rather than matters of life and death.

2. Women should fall in love because, not in spite, of a man's character.

3. Women who need to be so industrious absolutely must slow down; although it is very difficult, they are they are still obligated to seek the Now, for their own, as well as their loved ones, benefit.

4. Reading romances is not Reality.

5. Pleasant musical melodies of today may be harmless, but the words induce woman worship, and are not conducive to progress in the Way.

6. Just because Western society idealizes women does not mean that it is not misogynistic.

7. The most important thing for a woman in a relationship to discover is if she is being treated roughly, or solely as a sex object, by a blocked, or dehumanized partner, by describing the particulars of the relationship to her friends.

8. The challenge for women in particular, but also for men, is to not take to heart every thought, image, or feeling that rolls across the mind.

9. A material girl is a woman who has become so inured to sensation that she wants it all, and will settle for nothing less, when nothing, or the all in all, is what she should be seeking.

10. The vanity of a woman that is so difficult to overcome is derived from the fact that she knows that God creates through her alone, and that she must be perfect as a consequence of this amazing capacity.

11. Women know that men are less perspicacious, but err when they imagine they can recreate men in their own image.

12. Women are right so often that they are deceived into believing that they are always correct, that is a mistake; conflict between men and women may occur during the small percentage of the time when females are wrong.

13. A woman's loyalty to her man and children, while not spiritual, represents the highest possible human achievement in the active world of the senses; woman rises to the pinnacle of the species when she adds spirituality to these superior innate capacities.

14. While men may be slightly more creative that women, this fact is irrelevant to the Eternal Quest, as women can apply approximately the same will to do and know the good as men; creativity is not significant in the mystic's approach to meaning through inaction.

15. The advantage of women over men is in their self-contented, less striving or willful nature, but they must apply all the will that they have to achieve higher levels of Peace.

16. Because women are so loyal, they had better be very careful about the person to whom they fall in love.

17. It is easier for a woman to be a mystic without children, but there would be no more seers on planet earth without mothers.

18. A woman's loyalty to her mate must be chastened by

values and reason; otherwise, her love may become blind, and she may participate with him in immoral or irrational behavior, as minds mingle over time.

19. Women must work extra hard to progress in the Way, because the dedication to children, while most noble and altruistic, is ultimately materialist, and chains them to the material world, from which they must eventually escape.

20. Women whose friends encourage them to become more sexually promiscuous should find other friends, lest they become bored and impatient, and lose their femininity, as they become inured to a life of excessive sensation.

21. A woman who engages in excessive sensuality suffers more than one who has does not, without even being aware of it.

22. The problem with traditional society is that too many fine girls with great spiritual and moral potential have been given away by their parents to the wrong men for love of the more beloved dollar.

23. If a woman can rear her children with greater virtue without a bad husband, even in greater poverty, divorce is justifiable, because minds commingle, and the bad generally dominates the good, over time.

24. A woman should not remain with a man who enjoys inflicting subtle forms of mental and physical pain upon her, lest she become inured to abuse, lose common sense, and the way to the Spirit.

25. Women with low self-esteem should avoid relationships with men, as they are almost invariably abused in subtle ways; this unnecessary suffering also brings out the worst in their mates, and is morally harmful to them, by encouraging them to increased aggression.

28. Politics

1. The failure of Communism stems from the fact that its philosophers were too prolix in their writings, and their leaders too verbally loquacious in their speeches, to be of any use to anyone.

2. Politicians often seek higher office to get high on achievements that are usually far less than they imagine.

3. Everything in politics is comprehensible, except the degree to which insiders, international monopolistic capitalists, and bankers influence world affairs.

4. The most significant political decision a person should make is whether to be in favor of, or opposed to, the New World Order, or the end of nation states through globalization.

5. A belief in globalization should not be emotionally derived from envy of the United States and a desire to see it defeated.

6. Terrorism will slow, but not eliminate, the growth of globalization, as nation states take independent action to protect their security.

7. The fundamental causes of the planned or managed economy of globalization are the unfortunate excesses of the free enterprise system, that result from the belief of certain corrupt capitalists in profit at any price.

8. The only difference between political parties is that the Democrats tend to speed up the inevitable process of globalization, and the Republicans slow it down a little.

9. If it must occur, globalization should develop slowly, as the impoverished are integrated into industrial society, not rapidly, to prevent our collective life from devolving into mob rule, anarchy, and dictatorship.

10. Unfortunately, the price for world peace on the macro or political level, that involves the end of nation states, will be democracy and integrity in government at the very highest levels.

11. The era of small government is over; the larger the government, or bureaucracy, the greater the corruption.

12. Rather than say that all politicians are corrupt, measure the degree of corruption of a political candidate, and choose the one who is least dishonest.

29. Cults

1. Never join a group of unknown origin, or a strange religion, as it may be a cult; a cult can liberate the mind, but it takes possession of it at the same time.

2. Although they may rapidly break down ego defense mechanisms that prevent us from seeing Reality, cults are dangerous to physical and mental health, lead to cult leader worship, and are not a viable option in the Eternal Quest; layers of defenses must be removed slowly through meditation and vivid, transforming life experiences.

3. Cults are immoral because members are forced to bring other people into the group, who are often poor, to be duped and abused as well.

4. Large and well-known religious cults perfectly exemplify the self-contradictory and tragic results of spirituality without morality.

30. Religion: General

1. If the belief in God is a delusion, it is the mirage that is required for objectivity in life.

2. Ritual, an important part of religion throughout history, is meditative behavior that is meant to arrest negative thought and emotion by focusing the entire community upon neutral, habitual vocalization, and activity that has little ideational content.

3. Religion succeeds when it helps overcome the simple, mechanical provincialism of caring only for the family and small circle of friends, and fails when it stops at the borders of its followers.

4. A religion should reduce arrogance, or the belief in its own superiority to all other faiths; if it does not accomplish this simple and important goal, find another, more tolerant, denomination.

5. If one needs to be a part of something greater than oneself, satisfy that requirement through religion rather than politics.

6. "God visits the iniquity of the fathers upon the children unto the third and fourth generation of them that hate Him." (Exodus 34:7)

7. Regardless of the sins of our fathers, or our own natural moral disabilities, we are absolutely responsible for moving forward to become better people, and if we forgo this necessity, we may not go to hell, but we will live in it, or in unconscious ignorance, all the days of our lives.

8. Organized religion developed because spirituality is lost

without morality.

9. The less significant the religion, the less abstract its concept of God, and the more prominent are its sacred objects and holy men.

10. Love God only, and respect holy people as long as they are more spiritual and ethical than you, and can teach Divine Science anonymously, with humility.

11. Substantive spiritual entities and their holy icons, that divide Being into parts to satisfy the worshiper's need for objects of sense perception, often complicate, rather than facilitate, spiritual understanding.

12. Sacred objects and shrines of organized religion are of value in the Eternal Quest as long as one remembers that they are not meant to be worshiped, and pale into insignificance when compared to our glorious, pure, abstract, and non-material God, who deserves all of our love and attention.

13. Man is so object oriented and enmeshed in the physical world that he believes that even God should be understood through concrete attributes, description, and history, rather than more correctly through metaphor or high-level intuitive contact.

14. Those who founded the great religions– Moses, Jesus, Mohammad, and Gautama Buddha– were able to figure things out because they were either in the desert, or alone, and not distracted from feeling the presence of God.

15. The kingdom of God is within, but cannot be seen by busy people.

16. The battle of greater Mind over matter is the conflict between God and the devil, but Mind is always triumphant.

17. While theoretically salvation through God's grace is possible at any age, some of our youth today are so seeped in materialism that they become closed books at the age of twenty five, impervious to the influence of virtue, which only inspires their indignation.

18. Prayer is a fine expression of hope that may be effectual; simple communion with the Lord, or practicing the presence of God, achieves the same results, supernaturally and more efficiently, without the emotion and striving that often accompany formal supplication.

19. One cannot believe in the family in a vacuum, without church and temple, because caring for people outside the family usually cannot be properly inculcated without organized religion.

20. The way to get God to help you is to look at Him and love Him; give Him your time and attention, and He will give much more back to you.

21. God demands your complete, undivided attention, so you must be very still and silent to feel His holy presence.

22. With God all things are possible, but less probable, as sin continues unabated over the years.

23. Organized religion is correct when it says, "Science, next to values most dear."

24. Formal religion is valuable, important, and necessary, but is unfortunately often a defense mechanism against direct contact with God.

25. Many religious people are not hungry for God, but thought, and believe that He can only be known while in thought, which is a fallacy.

26. Religion concentrates a little too much upon words, thoughts, and speech, rather than upon just allowing people to feel God within and without; it is best not to always read, think, speak, or sing away the experience of God.

27. God is loved and praised in a perfunctory manner in organized religion, but one should strive to love and praise Him in a more direct and personal way, without words.

28. The sun has been worshiped for ages, and rightly so, as it is the greatest necessity of Life or Being in the universe.

29. Judaism is an ethnic and social religion that is based upon statutory or legal ethics: If you obey the laws, including commandments that may seem irrational, you will be blessed by God.

30. Religious Jews read sections of the Old Testament every week, over and over from year to year, and this ritual, which reminds them of how God manifested Himself on earth to their benefit, may be soothing and restful for the soul.

31. In both Judaism and Christianity, a high value is placed upon book learning that should not confer greater esteem upon seekers who excel in this area, for study is of value only in so far as it increases our love of God and man, and many achieve these lofty and wondrous ends with fewer words.

32. Yoga and Buddhism are insufficiently moral, but superbly spiritual; Christianity has the finest ethics, but is too oriented toward the personhood of Jesus, rather than the Holy Spirit.

33. The truly religious try love all people equally, rather than only members of their own particular faith.

34. God cannot change the past, but He can always neutralize its ill effects.

31. Religion: Christianity

1. God is the personification of the Present, and Jesus is the personification of God, and these more concrete representations make the Now less abstract for the benefit of the public.

2. The Spirit of Jesus is more important than his life in time, because the significance of his life is to impart the Holy Spirit to man.

3. Because he lived on such a high level of Being, Jesus Christ was not disturbed by the activities of the world below; thus he serves as a good role model for mortals like us who strive to overcome the reactive mind, and begin to live on the more elevated plane of Life.

4. If God is Love, or the Way, Truth, and Life, doesn't it make sense to make a little time for Him in your life?

5. Prayer and bible study are an essential means to instill integrity and conscience in children.

6. The bible is always good for reading and study; it is not useful to debate and defend a particular position on interpretation, as everyone has his own personal approach to the holy writ.

7. When one considers the corruption today, in all walks of life, one should run, not walk, to the local church, for a good, solid dose of morality, lest one ends up like our less fortunate, valueless brethren.

8. Religion must provide for the inculcation of good values in a calm and rational, rather than an excessively forceful, boisterous, or bible beating manner.

9. The grace of God is Peace, the alpha and omega of Christianity in its best and most abstract manifestation.

10. If one cannot admit one's mistakes to oneself or others, one lacks the requisite humility to confess one's sins to God.

11. We are all sinners, but some are a more sinful than others, and should be understood as such, and forgiven; the fact that we all sin should not be an excuse for a lack of discrimination between degrees of sinfulness that would only lead to a hypocritical rationalization for sin, and a mockery of forgiveness.

12. Most of the best pastors integrate meditation into Christianity, but do not tell their flocks that they are followers of the philosophy of the Now.

13. In Christianity, every pastor has his own personal interpretation of the bible, but contends that his approach is the only valid method dictated by the text; this often leads to vanity, or an unhealthy implied criticism of any other path to knowing what a particular passage means.

14. Christianity should begin with Jesus and end with Christ, but, unfortunately, for the vast majority of Christians, this magnificent faith begins and ends with Jesus.

15. The strengths of Judaism and Christianity are in the community they foster, and the good values they espouse; the weaknesses of Judaism and Christianity are the excessively materialist concern for the past of the former, and the past and future of the latter.

16. Catholics disenchanted by the indiscretions of their church should join a different Christian denomination; do not use the unfortunate immoral behavior of a small number of priests as an excuse to become a secular pagan, and risk the loss of good values cultivated over many years.

17. Despite the limitations of Christianity, with its convoluted and somewhat materialist metaphysic, it is unlawful to criticize this august religion unduly.

18. What is the profit of a Christian who imagines he is saved because he believes in salvation through Jesus, but behaves immorally; what is the merit of a meditator who achieves a higher level of tranquility through deep and prolonged concentration, but is unethical?

19. The paradox of Christianity is that God forgives sin, but one must absolutely not transgress His laws.

20. The key to Judaism and Christianity is avoidance rather than forgiveness of sin.

Made in the USA
Monee, IL
07 July 2026